I0840953

QUEEN BEE

by Karen Kellock Ph.D.

Manual for Superior Men

**A complete theory based on Einstein physics,
Political Psychology, Systems Theory
and Archetypal Psychiatry.**

FORMULA

**All success attraction
All disease obstruction
All recovery elimination**

You must fast on all three

OBSTRUCTIONS:

**People
Habit
Food**

QUEEN BEE

She brags about how she's a modern avatar then lets some joker she just met drive her car. What distinguishes a queen from the others is a sense of direction that shuts out losers & mean mockers: they aren't confused/indecisive virtue signalers.   Living without clarity is walking thru a mine field without caution--you're hurt badly if not trained soon. Brainless females use sex for manipulation: life becomes a cruel thing when there's no boundaries or direction. Silly women laden with sins taken in by wicked men in their own homes: I was one.

QUEEN BEE

QUEEN BEE

PUSH PEOPLE AWAY
EXPECT A SYSTEM INVERSION
LAY A BOUNDARY OR BE SORRY DARLING
THAT CRAZY FEELING AIN'T LOVE
NO MORE BEING ECLIPSED BY MAN
LOGIC OF UNREALISTIC LIBERALS
THEY WON'T PUSH THEIR MINDS
SELF-LOVE IS NOT NARCISSISM
HOME IS ALL
WRETCHED PATH OF WRITERS
HOME LIFE MAKES IT ALLRIGHT
RECAP OF QUEEN BE: ME
QUEEN BEE
IT'S ALL CONTINUOUS SOCIAL
DASHINGLY HANDSOME THEN A BUM
FLUSHING OUT EVIL ELEMENTS
SIN BREAKS HEDGE OF PROTECTION
THE SLAVERY OF SMALL MINDS
EVIL BOYS
PREVALENT PORN ATTITUDE
NO FLIRTING JUST SEXTING
ORAL SEX THEN A KISS
BOUNDARIES ARE A NARC-REPELLANT
WEAKNESS TRIGGERS ABUSE
ESCAPING SECRET COALITIONS
RUTHLESS AND JEALOUS
"MICROAGGRESSIONS"
YOU ARE NOT MY FRIEND
APPEASEMENT NEVER WORKS
MICROAGGRESSIONS ARE INVISIBLE
PREPARE FOR RACE WAR
REPRESSIVE TOLERANCE HURTS
THE GREAT DEAL TO KILL THE WEST
GO

QUEEN BEE

GOD THINKS HE'S AN ARROGANT CREEP
POLYMORPHY: BLURRED LINES
FIFTY-YEAR LIBERAL NARRATIVE
LIBERALS ARE PARROTS
TREATMENT MEANS DEBASEMENT
THE LEFT PROTECTS MUSLIMS
TRUMP DOESN'T OFFEND ONE BIT
TRUMP'S NOT A RACIST YOU TWIT
KEEP PROBLEM GOING FOR MONEY FLOWING
AMERICA STARTED WITH GUNGRABBING
DEMOCRATS DESTROYED INNER CITIES
WIMPY HUSBANDS TAKE VIEWS OF FEMINIST WIVES
LIBERALS SEE SHARIA AS PROGRESSIVE
LIBERALS SEE IMMIGRANTS AS VICTIMS
MOST LIKED ARE MEANINGLESS SITES
SEXUAL ASSAULT: "I'M NOT GOOD ENOUGH"
GANGSTER CULTURE PRIMING FOR PRISON
PATHOLOGICAL LIARS AND THIEVES
CONSERVE YOUR ENERGY/MAINTAIN IDENTITY
WHO ARE YOUR TRUE SISTERS? GOD-LOVERS
GOD VS. DEMOCRAT'S VOTER FRAUD
REVITALIZATION MOVEMENTS AND NATIONS
LOSE RESPECT FOR FANS OF TRASH
DIRTY SECRETS OF THE POWERFUL
CORNY COMICS PAID BY GLOBALISTS
LASCIVIOUS LIBS SEXUALIZE KIDS
FEMINISTS ARE THIRD RATE THINKERS
HILLARY WANTS TO KILL PRE-NEWBORNS
ALL-BULL FEMINISM LOOKS DUMB
FAKE NEWS: PROPAGANDA FOR AN AGENDA
FEMINISM MAKES WIVES COLD
HANDSOME LEADER BY WHAT HE DOES
HEALTHYMINDEDNESS

Preface
QUEENLINESS

I'm not choking just contemplating: do I want to be seen? Anonymity is keen.

Like bragging about how she's a modern avatar then letting some joker she just met drive her car.

We may be born pure but swim in muddy waters and it takes years to get clean or just a prayer.

WHAT IS A QUEEN?

What distinguishes a queen from the others is a sense of direction that shuts out botherers.

Shutting out botherers & mean mockers is seen as anti-social rudeness but she doesn't care.

Queens aren't confused nor indecisive. They're not mealy mouthed virtue signalers/passive.

Living without clarity is walking thru a mine field without caution--you're hurt badly if not trained son.

Brainless females not knowing how to handle situations may unconsciously use sex for manipulation.

Life becomes a cruel thing when there's no direction, boundaries or parameters: imagine it girls.

Below average women live with no vision, purpose or interest in politics. Just wake up/be cute.

Below average females the bible calls "silly women" laden with sins and diverse lusts/sin.

QUEEN BEE

Silly women are taken in by unscrupulous men who hypnotize them in their homes: I was one.

AVERAGE/BELOW AVERAGE FEMALES

Average women by contrast may have a goal but they vacillate in indecision, undirected by morals.

They have the target and gun in hand but won't pull the trigger and fall back from being unclear.

A double minded man/woman is unstable in all ways. They zigzag in confusion and misfire ok.

She accepts poor treatment from a clown then says "I'm a queen". They're unstable: that's what I mean.

They're unstable and unclear yet they think they are making them doubly dangerous I declare.

Therefore their life and outcomes are unstable. The divorce judge gave em 10%, now it's fatal.

The cruel instability living under a female tyrant cannot be understated I've said in many rants.

Unstable: Make a decision then switch with someone she talked to: the shifting sands of cookoo.

CLUELESS FAUX QUEENS

"I'm a boss queen" then she spends all her money on valueless stuff to show in selfies: how tough.

Struggling financially due to poor choices made just to impress. Mansions and anti-depressives.

You're not clear, you're addicted and double-minded thus you have no finesse or refinement.

QUEEN BEE

Clarity: You know who you are, where you're going and what you deserve. Clear, we start from there.

Stop introducing yourself by how much you've been thru. We all have a history/skeletons too.

Know what you want, what you DON'T want, and what your Creator says: I love and will prosper you.

Hard lessons taught me what I don't want: invasion, imposition, expectation, people dropping in.

UNFAITHFUL FRENEMIES

Unfaithful frenemies gossiping behind my back, perverse triangles, virtue signallers: bad.

Goals: to write/paint/sing with success. Free of distraction & detractors you just move into place.

An unstable woman may have goals but her house is a pit stop for losers and she never says NO.

An unstable woman will have sex with men even with her kids in the house. Immoral is NO BOSS.

An unstable woman will stalk men on the net, wasting valuable time in a chase as low as it gets.

A queen is too busy for this and won't self-demean. Men chase her--she does not chase a he.

Any time you stalk a man get angry at yourself, see how degrading it is and come back to senses.

Clarity promotes progressive action. "Write the vision so he man run that readeth it": she impacts em.

The vision is for an appointed time to speak and not lie. Though it tarries, wait for it WILL come, aye!

QUEEN BEE

WORK AND WAIT: VISION STAGES

Work and wait. Can she do that? No she fills her time with social/reactions to interruptions: fact.

A queen communicates vision for her life in stages, then manifests it when the appointed time arrives.

The queen/above average woman is a VISIONARY. She takes progressive action cuz she has clarity.

A woman's lack of clarity promotes stagnation, abuse and manipulation. That's a clear given son.

As a visionary a queen sees it, can present and explain it and then is motivated to run behind it.

Who you are, why you are and where you're going. The queen is able to FOCUS on these things.

QUEEN CHARACTERISTICS

Firstly a queen is clear on the lessons learned. She does not go back after seriously burned.

Queens learn from their mistakes and they shift--no foolish consistency when clear it missed.

Women have a low C factor: never learning from mistakes. It's over, over & over again ok.

When are you going to learn? Why you still in the middle of this? Why no shift with the last mess?

Queens don't just go thru problems, they grow from them. The others don't, they just repeat em.

A below average woman never learns from her experiences and thus she never advances.

QUEEN BEE

She chooses the same kind of man she calls "swag" with the same outcome: no queen hon'.

You were 18 now you're middle aged and choosing the same kind of man: unclear, no queen here.

I went from the rabble who held me back to a man who didn't drink nor smoke and was a Christian.

QUEENS LEARN AND SHIFT

Queens learn from their mistakes and SHIFT. They go thru nothing without learning of the pits.

She complains that men are dogs but then continues to put herself in the same position/godless.

She doesn't have to repeat the class cuz her notes from her education say: don't go that way.

A quiet rebuke to one of good sense does more than a whack on the head of a fool. Prov 17: 10

A fool never learns the lesson but a wise one changes course with just whispered instructions.

You can learn from what dad said or from experiences which are very painful, dreadful, lethal.

If you have to go thru it again & again it will break you down see: an epidemic of empty self-esteem.

A queen learns her lesson the FIRST time then gets right in line with her vision with energy, aye.

She repeats the same cycles, without a revelation of who she is and what she deserves [vital].

QUEENLY BOUNDARIES AND LIMITS

QUEEN BEE

A queen knows her limits. She's not confused about when she's had enough and eliminates it.

She learns the lessons but does not belabor them. She forgives and goes on without PTSD son.

The more you submit the worse it gets. Whether tyranny or bad relationships you must resist.

The queen's limits are her standards. Love aside, nothing pushes her beyond them ever.

If she's degraded and keeps showing up for it she's a woman who doesn't know who she is.

A woman who doesn't know who she is will be invaded constantly and if made worse left to die.

If no autonomy/boundaries early these invasions are accepted as bleak reality to be "pleasing".

"I'VE REACHED MY LIMIT"

"I've reached my limit"--period. Because the one thing she can never compromise is herself.

Going beyond her principals or values to please someone else means disgust of herself.

I can't compromise my standards for anybody cuz at the end of the day I gotta be able to love ME.

She keeps giving in to him as her morals degrade to nothing but she hates herself so it's ok see.

I can never love someone so much that I allow them to push my limits see--it begins/ends with me.

Between a queen and the others that's the difference: she will **NOT** be pushed beyond her limits.

QUEEN BEE

A queen says: I'm not comfortable with your kissing and hugging right now, while the others appease.

The way a man gets hooks into a woman's soul is by pushing her beyond her limits until she falls.

Once pushed beyond her limits she loses control of herself, that's how the devil's device works.

PUSHING HER SEXUAL LIMITS

Unscrupulous men will push a woman beyond her limits sexually so then he has total control see.

The woman won't go beyond 2 so he pushes her to 3 and eventually ten—no queen there then.

The queen goes to two and says "I'm not going any further" and he knows she means it too.

"Well you'll never get another man" and the queen says "so be it, this is as far as I'm going Sam."

Queens are clear on limits reached and lessons learned. You'll never be the same again, you discern.

You can't be clear on **LIMITS REACHED** until you have the clarity of knowing who you are see.

A queen knows what she deserves/where she's going so the perversions aren't happening.

A queen rests in her femininity and the right man must allow her that but today that's all mixed up.

It's not about baking cookies but far deeper: as a helpmate cuz man can't live without her.

She is created to help not initiate. Helping is connecting from her feminine to someone great.

QUEEN BEE

For a queen to rest in her feminine it must be a certain kind of man. She insists a man lead the clan.

NO TOUGH FEMINIST TYPES

A queen won't break a man down/belittling him as we see everywhere with tough feminist harridans.

If a man is interviewing for a relationship with her she's gonna insist that man leads for sure.

A queen conscious woman will never be fulfilled or happy with a man who can't lead ok.

But true leaders can also follow. Trusting her ideas he doesn't always have to initiate you know.

A queen doesn't respect a lazy man sitting around while she fixes all the issues nor a gigolo too.

Events, soul ties & strongholds attach like barnacles on a ship--dangerous nonessentials to rid.

A queen starts new each day, no past relics to degrade her energy and make her crazy with memory.

So this happened and that, even murder. You must work it all thru till it degrades you further.

LEISURE, FORGIVENESS, STRESS

Example: Joyce Meyers, raped 200x by age ten. She forgave to go on and look at her now hon'

A lady/genius/queen knows when to take the day off knowing leisure triggers creative clout.

She paints fingernails saying "I should do something useful" then forgets it with the next phone call.

QUEEN BEE

99.4% of Twitter employees are democrat donors. Is it any wonder we've been constantly censored?

FORGIVENESS GETS HIM OUT

See forgiveness as meaning "out". Forgive then they leave your soul, don't forgive = it's a block.

Two things form us: our genes and environment history. The latter changed me radically, forever see.

A queen doesn't have as many suitors as an average woman any man could be comfortable with.

A woman who knows where she's going puts a demand on a man: LEAD, so I can rest in my feminine.

I had the superior genes now I needed to tame the environment of lechers, imposers and fiends.

If I gotta take care of this and that cuz you're a couch rat how can I be happy and feminine man?

A woman is built to help but he never gets real help until he has a queen conscious woman giving it.

A below average woman won't put enough pressure on him to help him. This takes boldness man.

IRON SHARPENS IRON

Iron sharpens iron: the below average isn't built of the stuff so the man stays ordinary/boring.

She will never insist he lead and will take over when she gets the chance having no set boundaries.

How are you feminine when allowing a man to talk to you like that? Show up drunk/you still open up.

QUEEN BEE

A queen can't function in dysfunction. She's made to help a man/be his prize but not if weakened.

It's horrible to be the prize not knowing it while treated like a trinket. His behavior: she checks it.

HER MAN MUST LEAD

She can't rest in her feminine with he who will not lead or who is dishonorable, that's all she knows.

A woman's grateful submission is the natural reaction when receiving honor from her man.

Honor is the seed and submission is the fruit but it's all based on trust impossible with the callous.

A man who is dishonorable is never trustworthy so she can never truly rest in her feminine see.

She can't be feminine being like a cat in a roomful of rocking chairs or a grenade range of fear.

He's not a leader and he's not trustworthy. That man will NEVER allow her to rest in femininity.

Any dishonor she tolerates indicates she's not a queen and she'll see the results: he gets mean.

RESTING IN HER FEMININE

She needs to trust him to stay in her feminine so he can finally be a truly happy/successful man.

Superior females are clear on this dynamic. It's so important her marriage depends on it.

Queens are clear on who fits in her life. She doesn't force something that's not working, aye.

QUEEN BEE

She's only clear on who fits her life when she HAS a life in and of herself. Once knowing that, get out.

She must have her own independent existence first then see who fits that, never adapting to misfits.

She'd be the last to force relationships to happen, just to think of that would be so embarrassin'.

The below average fits people into her lowlife and just creates a pool of toxic sisters and strife.

A queen conscious woman is clear on who fits her life. She is soft steel, the tender glove, no strife.

CLARITY ON WHO FITS

Queens are clear on who fits their lives. Can two walk together except they agree? Amos 3: 3

Why force a situation that does not agree? Is there anything more discordant you can see?

You have nothing in common with him/those people and you're trying to force it? Never with evil.

She calls herself a queen but notice how unselective she is, a social butterfly or promiscuous.

It simply does not fit. No queen will force the fit or make a relationship work, that's a curse.

Would a superior woman whimper over an emotionally unavailable man? Never--not happenin'

Rather than wasting years on a cold guy in strife she says "no no, sorry, you don't fit my life".

Sorry, you don't fit my life, best to you, good luck in all endeavor, I'll be praying for you, good bye.

QUEEN BEE

No good woman forces a relationship with a mental mismatch and she'd never need a crutch.

There's no possible contribution he makes that could possibly intrigue such a woman, ya think?

Queens won't attach to a man who's only a spiritual sabotage, a sponge, a lover of the couch.

QUEENS REJECT SHIT TESTS

Some men give shit-tests calling you gabby, yappy or dirty: PASS the test by tossing him see.

If he likes rock n' roll screeches from hell and you like chillout take it as a sign it won't work out.

If your suitor turns on screeches from hell and the cacophonous crap rings your bell, swell.

So chillout is heavy on bass, so what. It's better than cacophonous screeches from hell: rock.

Things like that--his selections. Take note: is he just going along with the fads of his generation?

No queen goes for tattoos cuz God said don't mark up you body as the heathen do [it's ugly too].

She won't entertain a spiritual sabotage nor destiny delayers--wasting time with losers/hangers.

Because queens know who fits their lives. That's the most important thing: the right recipe, aye.

Most importantly, queens are clear on financial feasibility, not "why worry over the money?"

It's called inflation, price tags, quality of life, keeping things going smoothly despite outer strife.

QUEEN BEE

Falsehood: it doesn't matter how cruel he is if it's explained by an abusive childhood.

FINANCIAL FEASABILITY

A queen doesn't make money the main thing but a necessary foundation in the relationship.

She doesn't choose him necessarily for his money but his work ethic and vision--where is he goin'?

What is he working on now and where is he going? She either joins him or rejects the whole thing.

She sees him grinding every day and despite low figures he's gonna grow, she sees that clearly ok.

She's not gonna connect with one without financial discipline, work ethic or working a vision.

For her/the children she's not gonna launch into the future with a man who is financially uncertain.

Recap: He doesn't have to be rich but he has to have a work ethic, be an earner and have a vision.

Since queens are clear financial feasibility is a must they won't even move further with a chump.

A feast is for laughter and wine maketh merry but money answers all things the bible says.

Most of the psychological issues go back to the fact they didn't have money and it was sad.

Don't complain about it to the pre-marital counselor, a queen would surely have noticed it before.

QUEENS REJECT DRIP DRY HANGERS

QUEEN BEE

If all a man wants to do is hang at your house/eat outa you frig/sleep in your bed, reject him fast.

You each bring what you are to the table and together you multiply and build: that's normal.

1 + 1 = 20,000. Two are better than one for they have a good reward for their labor. Eccl 4: 9.

Queens are clear on other people's energy. They discern everybody and back off instantly.

Because queens are clear she gently and quietly removes herself from mismatches/fear.

It's fashionable to hate Trump when you don't know what you're talking about, Elmer Fudds.

Men took advantage of my hospitality when I was unclear on my destiny and limits see.

Memory shouldn't mean constant pinpricks but with someone with PTSD it does and life sux.

Just say: Thank you God for saving me without letting me ruminate on the awful incident see.

It's at a high price cuz you're a good writer. Now just leave everything alone and finally retire.

PH.D. IN THE STREETS

I don't hate you, you were my Ph.D. in the Streets. Cuza you I wrote a social psychology series.

Even back then they were insisting on pronouns he and she and it was all so illogical I went crazy.

New theories were giant speedbumps to my delivery, my reality imploded and then they drugged me.

QUEEN BEE

This was in 1976 so I can imagine the universities now with the planned creation of mental illness.

They put me on SRI's, I became a different person and lost my positions & grants: this was serious.

I felt like I was journeying thru the underworld--the underbelly of everything bad a shady.

The SRI's affected me for decades as an empty vessel 'til God recreated me on the Potter's Wheel.

OLD BOREGO

Instead of resenting your painful lessons notice how tough you are now and forever--thank em.

In my Ph.D. in the Streets it sickened me how wild, immature, callous and irresponsible they were.

They were invasive, entitled, overbearing, gross and wild. I never knew men lower than animals.

I was like an inmate jailed with thousands of wild immature humans see and it formed me.

I didn't have a house to protect me from the world I had to endure these folk and it really hurt.

The level of disgust is the height of your wall and that's how I am now: I've learned all I needed to.

When God considered me done on the wheel he yanked me outa Borrego to my reward/gated mansion.

I learned to look past the dusty shack to the ALL, the 1000 acres around me of nothing but God.

God saw I was happy in a dusty shack so he gave me double and I was equally happy with that.

QUEEN BEE

Finally all that crap from the herd--the constant need to explain/defend myself--was gone for sure.

Finally all that crap from the herd--the constant need to explain/defend myself--was gone forever.

WOMEN AND POLITIX

Most women say "I don't get into politics" but they're highly vocal about the issues: silliness.

There ain't nothing good about effects of feminism on the family, when you're living with cruelty.

Man just wants peace, home and tranquility but then the female needs to upset things see.

Debra was really mean to Raymond showing the evil effects of feminism and it isn't funny man.

The time Debra slammed a bowl of ice cream in his crotch--so female violence is ok or not?

In Everyone loves Raymond female violence is condoned and weak male fear of women is underscored.

Rest assured the new life will be the opposite to the old miserable one--for your approval they'll all run.

Prayer for serenity: "Sort it all out Lord, sort it out--so everyone sees what you want em to see".

"Act your age" doesn't mean to get a rocking chair but to be mature for a change: give us a break!

I put a bee in his bonnet and he gets right on it. A very useful process and problem solving habit.

MEMORY PIN PRICKS

QUEEN BEE

Feel a toxic memory then ask the Holy Spirit to remove the stronghold inside that evokes it see.

The devil lodges in our system and controls us thru hot memories like little stabs, stabs, stabs see.

Like the time I lent you 100 dollars and never saw you again. Little stabs out of nowhere of sin.

Make the decision you're not gonna keep hurting over an event in history you never stop feeling.

An event 30 years ago keeps coming up: Attack that: ask the holy spirit to remove the alien glob.

God doesn't want you to be pinpricked all day long with old memory relics: that's just for lunatics.

Free speech is number ONE see: Twitter stock will triple honey so that's where to put your money.

Here it comes again: that memory evoking adrenalin, guess you're a junkie on chemical triggerin'

One gets addicted to the chemical frenzy from that angry memory and his life is stuck see.

And in the case of anorexia nervosa, it is environmental trauma triggering genetic markers.

Don't pray to rid a soul tie, you pray the holy spirit removes everything in you attracting the guy.

They have Jesus Christ in their title but worship their apostles. The traditions of men: obstacle.

The left's monopoly on their warped view of the truth is over. Shadow bans have been lifted forever.

They emotionally manipulate audience to a preordained conclusion and they blindly accept it son.

QUEEN BEE

Elon Musk bought twitter, CNN is shutting down, Disney is reined in--it's a bad time to be woke friend.

A conservative is for family, religion, borders, defense, low regulation and freedom from the feds.

A liberal hates family, military, religion; wants open borders, high regulation and is authoritarian.

Trump could never have been elected in 2016 without a free internet so by returning to it = triumph.

When Twitter becomes the free speech arm of the free speech party the truth will explode finally.

When they smeared us we lost the giant platform to fight back, now we have it you sad sacks.

This could be an epic day for free expression--when one big domino falls they all do: dominion!

FEMINISTS HATE FREE SPEECH: TWITTER

It's a totally game-changing event: a massive platform with a world audience for our rants.

Massive reach for free speech: If this is true our time has come even before the election siege.

An honest reflection of public opinion: Now we'll see what Americans think without censorin'.

Thru algorithmic manipulation they've given us a false view of public opinion then the dems won.

The market will go free speech and it's game over as we're rid of the censorious reign of terror.

It's a major game changer being a reversal of the entire mantra of woke capitalism, a great danger.

QUEEN BEE

Algorithmic manipulation helped justify fake news narratives and the hatred of conservatives.

Free speech could restore key aspects of our democracy in the news and info industries.

Think of it: ALL communications of all types were complete controlled by the liberal hypes.

An unfettered Twitter has enormous implications for the America First movement: now we're movin'.

Twitter is a critical battle reversing the course of the war. No more stranglehold on rising stars.

QUEEN BEE

QUEEN BEE

HEAL TO ATTRACT HIGHER

As we heal our vibrational pull changes. This is called affinization: what you'll attract son.

If he can't see your worth or how you would profit him then let him go and let a **NEW** door open.

If he can't see your worth and value to **INVEST** in you girl then move on, you need money and **NOW**.

Now that I have synaptic clarity I am replacing memories and the intrusive PTSD is leaving me.

Your husband says he doesn't care if the dishes pile up but he would if he hadn't mal-adapted to it.

It's the generation of broken consciousness. not having a clue what your value is and begging for likes.

WOMEN SHOULDN'T CHASE MEN

Broken, society convinces women they are slaves not rulers, that they have to beg for favors.

Begging for something that already belongs to you is broken consciousness, then disrespect.

Too many women today are in hot pursuit of men and the sad result is a dearth of commitment.

If something is readily available the value of that thing drops like a rock: why buy cow if free milk?

The man who deserves you will have enough motivation and energy to pursue YOU/commit too.
A real man takes pride in the fact he went after his prize and won. Pride is very important to a man.

QUEEN BEE

A real man won't take pride in the fact that "my wife ran me down and caught me and that's that".

A man wants to know he went after her and won see. Adam recognized Eve and took the lead.

FEMALE CHASERS ARE MASCULINE

When a woman pursues a man it's the manifestation of pure masculine energy and repels him.

It's a sliding interactional scale: the more masculine her chase the more feminine her new man is.

A feminine man does not want to lead and is content with being kept, a masculine man hates that.

If he doesn't have enough masculine energy to lead, honor and protect he's not your man see.

We will always attract the opposite to our energy. The female hunter will find the subservient see.

The conquered man is prey. Some may see that as cute but with time and life changes, no way.

A real masculine man will be afraid of an overly aggressive woman, it's a real turn off man.

The tough lady thing will repel what she wants and attract what she doesn't want, a cuck.

If she pursues a man she'll never attract one that is able to sustain her especially in the long run.

The strange woman flattereth with her words but her house is inclined to death as a curse.

None who go unto her return or take ahold of the paths of life. What she gets she can't respect, aye.

QUEEN BEE

And any man who would allow you to pursue does NOT possess true masculine energy Sue.

ALPHA MALES TURNED OFF BY THE HUNT

A real man works for the protection of womanhood but won't respond to a masculine female's hunt.

A woman in pursuit misrepresents her virtue. Is she loose or can she be committed in lieu?

When a woman is overly aggressive it makes him feel she lacks discipline and necessary restraint.

A pursuing woman lessens her value as a wife so he is less committed to her protection, aye.

"My clock is ticking" she says as the media spurs her on to get her man but to him it's sickening.

A virtuous woman sits back and allows the man to take the aggressive approach: to be masculine.

With a virtuous woman the man leads and she simply rocks with him tho' at times has objections.

CREATIVE CATALYST CAN BE FEMININE

He makes a move, she makes a move. But it's ok if she creates and for both sakes he behooves.

She's truly more of a woman than that but society's put pressure--desperation: she must act fast.

All she can do is concentrate on her own value/work then wait for her "husband" to act first.

When she's jumping the gun like that it degrades her virtue and she may even seem loose.

QUEEN BEE

A virtuous woman chasing a man? She's sending off the wrong signal which is opposing God's plan.

The two comportments [chase/wait] are an entirely different vibrational pull and I mean that girl.

I'm at my highest when the world is asleep. It's such a trip and the silence of solitude so sweet.

DESPERATION IS NOT VIRTUE

Desperation for relationship sends off the wrong signal girl. It is self-serving and not true virtue.

I know sisters, mother and aunts bug you to death and even question your head but wait instead.

I know your friends are married and you feel outed but work on thyself then enters Sir Galahad.

Wife is to be discrete/chaste [free of defilements or impurities] and that's all trashed by her chase.

When a woman pursues a man it's seen as desperation and it's exactly like bleeding in the ocean.

Blood in the ocean attracts sharks that will devour you. That is the result of your desperation Sue.

Desperation is lowered value. If her desperation shows the sharks come in right away/she's screwed.

Because he was old I assumed he was nice, a reflection of a sheltered childhood without advice.

THEY WAFFLE ON THEIR VIEWS

They waffle on their views so how can we trust em too? But one is firm about it--we join his crew.

QUEEN BEE

They're hot, they're cold, they waffle and zigzag. Mealy mouths and social manipulators: red flags.

When predators sense emotional weakness they swoop in to manipulate and take advantage.

They sacrifice facts to preserve a false narrative. It's an endless debate so don't engage the bible said.

Narrative: people of color can't be racist so when they shoot up white people, they deserved it.

Don't be a light switch where others have the power to bring you down suddenly as if bewitched.

Free thinkers bashed in families of mostly women: They collude/triangulate and get lawyers on em.

Left loves billionaires when building electric cars see--but turn on em for wanting free speech.

Women fear taking a stand. "I don't talk politics": to get approval/avoid disapproval of man.

PUSH PEOPLE AWAY

They ruin their lives by a compulsion to be social. It's an evil expectancy so the strong refuse it all.

Why are you destined to rule? Because you've been down, dominated and degraded by fools.

Healing occurs when you shift your focus from what happened to how you're handling it now.

Don't push people away with Loneliness Leaking. It spills out then they go away cuz you seem so needy.

If you've ever been around a narcissist you realize how fast they can wear you out as they persist.

QUEEN BEE

EXPECT A SYSTEM INVERSION

That's the early life of the leader but a **SYSTEM REVERSAL** shifts everything into high gear.

You know how to rule cuz you've learned what it's like to be their mule. This gives you empathy too.

Sin and the devil makes people look like fools--clowns and caricatures in puffy planes/protuberances.

To be the **BEST** leader you had to gain the **MOST** empathy and that came from humiliations and tragedies.

I've been through things involving people and systems that were excruciating, all so I could tell you.

Long periods of desert solitude where I saw no one for months then total bedlam when they'd come.

How inconsiderate the social generation is. You'd think it'd be the opposite but they really impose it.

LAY A BOUNDARY OR BE SORRY DARLING

If you don't lay a boundary they're compelled to impose on you to absurd limits, it's the devil in em.

Yah I'm really gone. I'm not interested anymore as my understandings brought a lack of heart throb.

The older human gives spectacular demonstrations of wit and zest, does his best work then he passes.

Suddenly it seems everyone in the health field is under 25. We're in a whole new world, no lie.

Yes you're in the Beginning of the End but it still doesn't mean anything, you could make a century.

QUEEN BEE

You just gotta take more naps, take your sups and re-align your maps. I'm up all night now, fact.

I have to thank my enemies for giving me the raw material for these 130 books on the new social psych.

That's the only way to look at it--make lemonaid not belly ache cuz the adversity is what made you great.

There is no "peaceful coexistence" between opposite theories of life, government and life-management.

Initially the narcissist does the "deep dive" into pseudo-empathy then later discards you as silly.

Tho' the narcissist seems indifferent he actually has Rejection Sensitivity to which he over-reacts.

He will deny the impact of abandonment not wanting to look weak but actually his reality turns bleak.

THAT CRAZY FEELING AIN'T LOVE

When you get that crazy feeling again, note it's NOT love but probably terror and listen to it friend.

Youth couldn't stand disagreement and they thought they owned me. No coping skills/coulda killed me.

Having no inner reality--from family dysfunction and immaturity--they had to control...ME.

Women are sensitive around the neck and shoulders so either we want [fake] fur or nothing there.

They impose themselves/think they own you. That's the social generation and I've had it up to here too.

There's nothing more exhilarating than payback day. It will come, just stay low and work in calm, ok?

QUEEN BEE

DON'T let em around your pets cuz they'll take em just to get a laugh--these creeps are cruel and cold.

Don't go back to who you fought to get away from. Mentally and emotionally it's so good now.

If you work for a big corporation can you think the way you want or do you adapt to how they think?

Too bad he can't keep up but really no one can when you think about it--need managers not sidekicks.

My generation was promiscuous but your generation is morally insane without lines which is worse.

Your whole ageist attitude made me feel old. You're Mr. Superior taking on the herd's reality dude.

The feminist says "sometimes you need a little prairie justice" and that justifies all her messes.

NO MORE BEING ECLIPSED BY MAN

Man, I turned a corner. I'm never coming back into that rut feeling like hell everyday just by knowing yer.

Satan's sneaky but don't let em in. He'll do anything to hoover you back like cycles in past/be firm.

You know what you can take and what you can't. You know your limitations and what you're best at.

The kids are vigilantes who will take prairie justice on anything causing upset: their new targets.

You can heal your mind thru comedy. I heartily laugh two hours a day with my favorite varieties.

LOGIC OF UNREALISTIC LIBERALS

QUEEN BEE

The logic of liberals is so reversed from reality and common sense it'll mess up your life friends.

With intrusive memories, think: "I'm having a PTSD attack" and that brings your center back.

Every generation has it's own reflection of the perverse crookedness of the human heart.

Don't blame them, it's what happens with sin. Everything is lost or leaves your side, sure as the sun.

The bible says it's healthy to LAUGH. I see it as therapy to enjoy comedy and what a relief every day.

He/she wasn't the one. Instead of crying you should be jumping up & down at what you saved yourself from.

The millionaire youths who don't answer to thine have crossed the line, worse than porn crimes.

It's always a backhanded comment from him. One way or another he let's you know that you're failing.

What is a life well-lived? It's maximizing innate talents for the good of those around you and I'm doing it.

THEY WON'T PUSH THEIR MINDS

If they won't push their mind to understand you then why be anxiously dependent on their approval?

My path to being a writer wasn't about writing but hurting deeply. After prolonged pain I had an opening.

I asked God to remove all thoughts of the past or people and He did--I feel so present/here and now.

If he can't understand you why would you need HIS approval? Seems to me you'd avoid the fool.

QUEEN BEE

SELF-LOVE IS NOT NARCISSISM

Big difference between self-love and self-centeredness. The former's good, the latter's a narcissist.

Making up your own truth as you go along or feeling superior to others--how can that be healthy?

The narcissist is deeply, pathologically defensive. When you love yourself this is not how it is.

When you love yourself you're open to nature, beauty, art and music. You're part of it all, not a lunatic.

When you love yourself you're compassionate and humble and can stand in your own goodness.

n acting out of "concern" it's really just a smear campaign--that's how the sneaky liberal causes pain.

To be a writer sometimes you sit in your swill and hurt deeply until it's a word-flood to eternity.

Until they come out of the fallen state, women are sluts and men are slut-makers. Jesse Lee Peterson

HOME IS ALL

I feel such sympathy for youth if they're not set up. An older woman has foundation: a warm house.

I miss you too but I can't take that crap. I'm not GOING to take it and you won't change so just accept it.

A smart wife makes her husband LOVE his home so he'll protect it, provide for it and want to stay in it.

A smart wife's husband never wants to leave home where he walks tall while the world goes to hell.

QUEEN BEE

I'm at the beginning of the end--not much time so hell if I'll waste it on your ups and downs friend.

All thru history a happy husband in his abode will go to war to protect country, family and HOME.

Home is ALL where we walk TALL. To be homeless is hell unprotected from elements and criminals.

Man builds home but woman is homemaker: household routines and the best ways of doing things.

A happy marriage is where every day's a holiday and every meal's a banquet so why fight it?

WRETCHED PATH OF WRITERS

It's not about "writer's block" but the personal growth I need to break through it--what a trip.

My path to being a writer was sitting & hurting in the desert wilderness for 20 years, THEN I wrote.

While in the desert without a fence I was imposed on by the dense so of course I'm walled in this.

While in the desert without a fence I was imposed on by the dense so of course I'm walled in like this.

My path to writing was figuring out why I'd gone from a palace to a shack/why my world went black.

Affluent liberals/bully pulpits leading whole generation of youth into gutter thinking it doesn't matter.

My path to being a writer was an ocean of tears. Trying to crack through whatever it was creating fear.

I barely made it out with my life. In retrospect I can see Jesus saved me many times from strife.

QUEEN BEE

Baptist lady insisted her grandson had nothing to do with the broken windows etc, and I should be nice.

I coulda been killed way out in the desert just cuz I wouldn't let people in my cabin--imagine.

It was a SOCIAL generation and that was expected unless you laid a boundary and meant it.

I'll admit I was crazy all through the process but a life's work finally shows brightly and I own it see.

Prolific Writing is cuz I held it in for decades and it BOILED and transmuted to gold, THEN I wrote.

HOME LIFE MAKES IT ALLRIGHT

He says "you don't have to take the nuclear option" but I say yes you do, going no-contact is just that my friend.

Now you have everything you need for a deliciously satisfying and thinning FRUIT and STARCH diet.

Rain, sleet and snow--I've never been so excited! Winter weather thrills me while I'm working inside.

Everyone's mother has hidden a sack of sugar for difficult times and that's the potent point, a real sign.

When day turns to night all I see is colored lights blinking all around--that's my decor all year round.

I have a right not to be violated in my "persons, houses or effects" but they're encroaching on us fast.

How Sleepy Joe sold us out totally, to everyone, for cash unlimited and nevertheless can become king.

RECAP OF QUEEN BE: ME

QUEEN BEE

I have a bad problem with PTSD but who doesn't in this generation, it's immorality imposing on women.

Women bashing president for "grabbing" when they're the most slutty generation we've ever had man.

We're not supposed to "slut shame" for that's being mean but that's what it is in the fallen state.

I had no idea how low people got. I assumed they all had orderly lives/would do what they said they would.

I coulda been killed. They talk of getting "hits" on each other and just that's a first step ending in hell.

Losers had no lines/scared me out of my mind. They were high school '85--so now what are they like?

Cuz of what high schoolers '85 did to me I have PTSD for life--what are they like now guys?

It was so horrible being imposed on by raucous/vacuous youth I'll be talking 'til my last dying breath.

If everything's about sex then everything's about sluts and slut-makers in the fallen state.

There's too much elasticity. When you fall to lower archetypes I don't know you and it's freaky.

When you became a caricature of a human/fell to lower archetypes it was so freaky to me man.

Get past the lustful attraction to the lower archetypes he displays at times, he's not steady hon'.

DASHINGLY HANDSOME THEN A BUM

Dashingly handsome at times then lookin' like a dam bum stinkin' to high heaven. Need consistency darlin'

QUEEN BEE

Repentance brings consistency--you're locked in a higher state, not going back to adolescent mates.

I was punished for my reactions to BEDLAM. I wanted order and a SHREEK came out I'm sure.

I don't want them coming into my house, where they split off and look into drawers and whatever else.

I'm scared to death of these people, they are horrible but Stockholm Syndrome makes us adaptable.

They imposed so much and were so presumptuous it made me a recluse for life even in marriage.

High school '85 went to prison cuz their Baptist grandma denied everything they'd be doin'

It was a land without justice where I was accused of doing everything they were doing with mocking.

When everything you think and create must be filtered thru HIM [the narcissist] forget it mate.

I'll never get over it. Maybe that's why God decided I wouldn't have kids, I woulda been a lunatic.

The mere fact he's elastic--from highest to lowest--shows he lacks the needed mature consistency.

QUEEN BEE

Queen Bee perfectly exemplifies the arrogance of liberals. So beyond the pale of entitlement, and soulless.

Police brutality is color-blind: more whites are killed than blacks. See the whole, know the facts.

QUEEN BEE

Haven't we had enough of these fakes, frauds, phonies and backsliders? Be rid of these posers!

A double minded man is unstable in all his ways. He's a liar and thief but bcuz we let him, crime pays.

True feminism: a woman defends herself. State-run feminism: weak, chip-on-her-shoulder, daft.

IT'S ALL CONTINUOUS SOCIAL

TV "Friends" was all social and this started the thinking it was "superior" to waste your time shooting the bull.

Conscience: I've read that the saints have "stinging remorse" while the wicked couldn't care less.

Remorse for past sins: It really wasn't us it was the devil who had the default position out of our weakness.

We've come to the point where we don't argue or try to reason with we just block or unfriend--that's how bad it is.

SOCIETAL SCHISMS: We're already there. People don't reason and debate they just block and hate.

FLUSING OUT EVIL ELEMENTS

We're reaching a crescendo and it's flushing out the evil elements. It's a good thing, just ban em.

TRUTH upsets people so now truth is illegal since all they care about is feelings--the emboldening of evil.

Saying "your words make me upset" is weaponizing emotion giving power to the most primitive manipulation.

Higher capacities: reason, debate, evidence. Now it's cry babies: tantrums/upset to dictate our speech!

QUEEN BEE

Just cuz you **FEEL** it doesn't give you the right to violate people's freedoms, but that's what's happening.

Like Atlantis arising out of the ocean that's the [genius] human mind when released from obstruction.

Delete a sentence on a computer and it's gone forever. In the same way our sins are erased and disappear.

I even think liberal relatives could snap. There is no more reason mediating stimulus with response: animals.

As a petite female 102 lbs I must withdraw. I can't object cuz don't wanna be hit and they have won.

The new matrix is based on emotion, not reason. That means no mediated response--they'll get violent soon.

The feminist bully in the family rejected easily and early if there was any discordance with her rigid reality.

SIN BREAKS HEDGE OF PROTECTION

Sin breaks down your hedge of protection. The evil world flows in and you're incapable of prevention.

Repentance brings back protection. Existence becomes comfy again and you embark on creation.

Women have become as violent and pugnacious as men. There is reason to fear them/don't push em.

If you love your pets don't provoke a fight cuz adversary will pick on them. Be wise, you're dealing with scum.

These are really creepy people and they're well paid to create bedlam. Fence up, dig in, protect pets/children.

Irrespective of what you said they hated you for the vibes you gave off. Inner conflict/sin = they mock/scoff.

QUEEN BEE

If you have the devil in you they'll react to him not you but it's a terrible collision nevertheless, you'll feel it lass.

Music is so much more profound and deep than watching political vids. I must remember that for bliss.

Animals: stimulus - response. Mature people: stimulus - sleeping on it, reasoning - response.

THE SLAVERY OF SMALL MINDS

The worst misery was small minds having power over me. That was my youth until I outlived em and was free.

The sinner is so out of grace he brings dysynchrony and others come against him--a natural discordance.

I can hear people yelling at me cuz I had the devil in me but even so it's a serious introject believe me.

A sinner is grasping--too much into his own cocoon to be any good and the tribe comes against him soon.

The repentant man has let all that go, he's more apart of the whole yet still separate: holy/in the know.

All I can do is continue to write and hope God rewards me tonight or even today if He gets the chance.

It's what He made me to do, He put the words in me so He'll also have the LINK ready on cue.

EVIL BOYS

Half of sex assaults on children are from adolescent boys, and the naive young girls are seen as sex toys.

Attitudes from porn: male dominance/female submission is the sexual paradigm and girls must accept it.

QUEEN BEE

Young people are not learning of intimacy, friendship and love but about cruelty and humiliation in porn.

Intimacy and tenderness is what girls want but they can never find the sensual slow-burn of real love.

Love: healthy equality, honesty, respect. Porn: domination, disrespect, abuse, violence and detachment.

Porn trains the consumer's brain to sexualize, objectify and dehumanize people--it's destructive and evil.

Solitude is healing, making life worth living. Talking is torment, I need days to recover. Karl Jung

PREVALENT PORN ATTITUDE

[1] Emotionally vacant sex orientation [2] the sick sexual expectations that follow, seen as contractual.

The porn attitude degrades the woman. She's gotta be strong to confront his nasty **EXPECTATIONS**.

If the Porn Attitude is not nipped in the bud society will collapse since **RUIN** is always about deviant sex.

Look at Sodom and Gomorrah--they were doing it in the streets all over town. Deviancy knows no bounds!

It is the biological drives that become compulsive, i.e. addictive. See Youtube's mukbangs of gluttony.

Food and sex--the two bio-drives which become perverse. Think of it: it's all about sex/eating too much.

I don't know how men of past eras controlled themselves but they did. Now **NO** control, it's just expected.

It's the **FEMALE** who must apply breaks, but find me one who can? She'd be called a fool/fear rejection.

QUEEN BEE

To be used and cast aside, I can't think of anything worse. Coldly degrading, never speak again or be cursed.

The sex thing is so overwhelming I don't even wanna talk about it but I have to, it's so oppressing us.

NO FLIRTING JUST SEXTING

How tough, how horrendous, how inconceivable it would be to be a girl today adapting to these boys.

No more flirting! When you like a guy you text your boobs, he texts back his genitals--that's called dating.

Other than weakness, none of it was your fault. You were assaulted by a mindset in which it was expected.

You were assaulted by a mindset and then you even said you LIKED it! But face it girl you NEVER did.

It was a DEGRADING expectation and you know it. Just cuz the whole culture does it doesn't nicen it.

Worst fear: small minds having power over me. That suffocating feeling of boys and expectancy.

ORAL SEX THEN A KISS

Expected to give oral sex before first kiss. Inoculate your girls against perverted male expectancy please.

Who is causing world problems and violence? Young boys, and it's the same for girls made into sex toys.

The boys view porn, the girls know it and in fear of rejection or for attention they usually conform.

The boys watch porn, the boys compare notes/pics, they expect oral then anal and you don't object?

QUEEN BEE

It's gone so far I don't know if they can learn tenderness, love and patience. They want it all **NOW.**

The lady said "it wasn't stuff you view, it was written smut but it hurt me just as much, I'm shocked!"

BOUNDARIES ARE A NARC-REPELLANT

PREY for narcissists: those afraid to set boundaries, who care what others think or are raised to cater.

Self-love with firm boundaries is a narcissist-repellant: lay a boundary and they'll disappear as irrelevant.

Take the time to heal childhood trauma/codependent behaviors. Fall in love with the true self forever.

Humans are very animalistic in their assessment of each other. Devalue yourself and you're dumped.

How do we train ourselves to stop leaking that energy by thinking of an ex or hankering over the past?

The less of an "I" you have the more of a delicious desert you are to a narcissist. Love yourself first.

To escape the narcissist you gotta build yourself up and realize that sometimes you must fight back.

WEAKNESS TRIGGERS ABUSE

It wasn't that you were so wrong but that your weakness triggered their abuse like they were on top.

Never make decisions based on your emotions especially with children. Regarding their pets, don't use em.

Their pets are their first love object and you have **NO** right to punish them by pet-rejection or execution.

QUEEN BEE

Dog meat is based on the same principal as adrenochrome from babies: both are tortured for beauty/jollies.

They look at aging as disease. Not the pinnacle of life or crown glory but a sickening thing without relief.

Imaginary monsters: they call em "microaggressions" cuz you can't see em. It's IMPLICIT bias, so hang em.

Due to your sins you were weakened and they could accuse you of anything. Repentant, that's not happening.

How dare you complain about looters and crimes when the police are still out there enforcing the law.

They'd eat your corpse after a week and sure they stay at your grave but that's duck-imprinting not real love.

They are pampered children play-acting at revolution and they're not courageous they're pathetic. Tucker

ESCAPING SECRET COALITIONS

I sensed the secret coalitions constantly and wanted only to flee. A lucky refugee I got protection by a he.

I will wait for you forever. It's just the way it is, we are birds of a feather.

Donald Trump's niece is ESTRANGED [pissed], that's why she bashes him like that: the system of brats.

Trump's niece has a trauma bond that compels her to put him down--to the whole world too, that's how profound.

The estranged black sheep's identity is so tenuous she MUST fight back--it's the way she remains intact.

Trump's brother--the author's father--was an alcoholic and that would mean she's screwed up too I gather.

QUEEN BEE

Chicago's murder rate up by 80% past month. But don't worry, Lori Lightfoot says it's just due to guns.

141% increase in gun violence in NYC but don't worry Mayor Bill De Blasio said "Who needs police?"

I still miss my cat. Maybe sister was right when she said I was over-attached but they were my escape from rats.

The unconditional love of an animal vs. the mixed signals, duplicity and treachery of people you've known.

Even neutered male cats roam. The females stay home so that's what we'll have, I can't go thru this again.

You love an adorable cat that much and then they're gone? I can't go thru this again, fix the dog door hon'

Stop putting down females and their cats. You're encouraging cat-abuse by exes the dirty rats.

RUTHLESS AND JEALOUS

I can't be part of a narc harem I'm number one or forget it man that's just the way it's always been, amen.

Mean liberals and Jezebels will take revenge thru the love of your animals. Watch this, it's common as hell.

These people are despicable: ruthless and jealous. There is no intervening variable between stimulus/response.

Mean ruthless mommy will punish Johnny by taking his pet away. This is the main EARLY TRAUMA I'd say.

I don't know whether it's fear of exposure, body dysmorphic disorder or just shyness but I'm purely a homer.

I figure words are enough: 51,000 tweets in 112 books on social psychology and how they screw us up.

QUEEN BEE

"MICROAGGRESSIONS"

Microaggressions: if you say anything deemed impolite in the mind of a young person it is called "racism".

The left does not wanna hear thoughtful disagreement. They won't even admit it exists, it's all irrelevant.

It's a triumph of ideas. A huge house you've built through the years. Multi-layers, maturity from errors.

Goodbye world, I've said it all. I can't stand it anymore cuz I'm a dinosaur and hate the low so go to hell.

Home to roost: decades of dung from criminal public schools breeding fools so now its bedlam cuz they're tools.

I had all these ideas but not the right way to express em so was just mad all the time/needed assertion.

24-hour computer life: GET AWAY FROM IT, you can pick it up any time--that's the point.

YOU ARE NOT MY FRIEND

You are not my friend. Go away I never wanna see you again. Disappear and stop imposing.

The Fallen Hero Syndrome can be a terrible thing as you fall into disrepute and everyone jumps on the boat.

When insanity took me over it was THEIR demons in me. I never wanted them around but was unfree.

When insanity took over and the house was brought down that was YOUR alcohol you brought around.

The liberal narrative instructs wives to put down men mercilessly and in front of others you see.

QUEEN BEE

When eclipsed by a Bad Mother Archetype I was mad all day and night. Forgiven and healed, it's all right.

APPEASEMENT NEVER WORKS

Appeasement: Unless you're willing to surrender everything you'd better surrender nothing.

Even Macron said "No you're not taking one little statue, you can go to hell-- it's part of our history."

This statue and stand-down thing has flushed out the wimpy wishy-washy enabling republicans.

Facebook censured me for saying it was cruel to eat a live animal--cultural relativism makes us sad as hell.

Once you realize life is a **WAR** you don't feel remorse for your negative reactions to liberals **ANY MORE.**

Liberals are so stupid they think that just cuz people are protesting it's true what they're protesting about.

July 4 should be loud celebrations for it's the most important thing: our freedoms.

CNN: "Mt Rushmore is by slaveowners on stolen Indian land" but they called it "majestic" when Obama went.

Tho' Hitler killed millions, Germans still have so much to be proud of in their history--it's the same thing hon'

MICROAGGRESSIONS ARE INVISIBLE

The notion of "microaggressions" was created because there **WERE** no blatant indications of persecution.

The **ONLY** openly racist activity we see in America is against white people. I'll say it again: **ONLY.**

QUEEN BEE

They started out against "patriarchy" but that's conflated and morphed to ALL white people who are guilty.

Who'd wanna be a part of them? Our cities are in ruin, devastated by radical Marxists ideology/scum.

Repressive tolerance: you condone and encourage all from the minority/put down and discourage majority.

The only way to coalesce disparate groups together was by creating a common enemy--the white guy.

How else could they join LBGT with the Muslim community? By creating their common enemy, you and me.

Just walking into their groups gave me the creeps. It was so sudden when falling into a hell run by women.

The liberal den of thieves and make-believes. They are always mean cuz it's the devil's scheme.

The dominant culture in the West Democrats thought they could destroy by a coalition of minority groups.

Made it fashionable to be black or brown and put down whites as ugly old clowns but we built Europe ya' know.

PREPARE FOR RACE WAR

Prepare for a race war, this ain't going away. It's happening secretly and in alley ways, a cruel destiny.

It's all coming home to roost: the results of fatherless homes and not going to church: monsters.

Repressive tolerance: tolerate ALL liberal views of minority, repress/ban ALL conservative views of the majority.

How to keep the coalition of the oppressed together: blame the white guy for everything even the weather.

QUEEN BEE

Splitting the party: after putting all their hopes on a coalition of the oppressed blacks will go to [R] Kanye West.

As blacks follow Kanye West Dems collapse cuz they're no longer a viable force without the coalition of oppressed.

It's a WIN: if Trump remains the Outsider, the Disrupter and the Change Agent for his voters.

REPRESSIVE TOLERANCE HURTS

We've all been touched by this psychically, if not personally. We all see the darkness of this reality.

I want the news not boobs. Fox news and even Alex Jones is guilty of using sex to sell to fools.

Our main problem is low-information voters. Mainstream news like CNN and MSNBC are lie-promoters

Did your friends/family enable one of the worst criminal takeovers (of our great America) in history?

Weakness arouses evil. That's all we've gotten from the left's "leading from behind": think, people!

Obama was planning "dissident extractions" first--take you away. If no Trump, darkness takes over, ok?

THE GREAT DEAL TO KILL THE WEST

The deal's been made to kill the west/shut down true liberalism and is orchestrated by liberals (social fascists).

He called out Newt for what he said rather than the perpetrators of the tragedy killing 83 dead.

They create the environment that creates the conflict and then they escalate it--hard to believe it?

QUEEN BEE

An assault on law enforcement and open season on decency: the bikers are addressing the tragedy.

Now that it's popular they'll go along with it. They are leafs in the wind--soulless--and I'm sick of it.

What about all the babies killed by these creeps? They'll never be clean again (unless repent, please!)

It's not just about criminal Hillary but all your friends who went along with her--to the pillory.

A win over Obama/Hillary with a Trump ascendency is a settling of all old doubts/scores and more!

GOD THINKS HE'S AN ARROGANT CREEP

God thinks he's an arrogant creep too! He will take care of this as the Vindicator (don't be blue).

Martial Law beginnings are called "war games" and that's why they're on the streets, they claim.

What do we want? State's rights. The more local the less devil so just that increases our heights.

Black Liars Murder (BLM) is the result of Pres. stirring the pot then appointing himself to mop it up.

Cops make 12 billion a year taking your stuff/money. Policing for profit's a huge industry honey.

Civil forfeiture happens in all states. Eating our substance/taking our stuff puts us in dire straights.

Obama pretended--responding to the situation he created to provide pretext for takeover he wanted.

Melanis outclassed Michelle Obama and thus the media's gone insane (at the people's chosen reign).

QUEEN BEE

We have a right to feel safe! But they've made that impossible—as evil exists (but with Jesus we are saved).

The republican platform sought to block slavery and Lincoln was the rep defeating it with the military.

POLYMORPHY: BLURRED LINES

Polymorphy is: blurred lines, having many mates. It's a sign of the end times: indecency and hell's gates

The cost of Hillary's dishonesty could be the loss of America as we know it. Newt Gingrich

When Trump gets in we'll be rid of the divisive liberal media: censors, critics and cynics.

The media/politicians will do and say anything to keep their rigged system in place. Donald Trump

Potential vanishes into nothing without effort. Donald Trump

What we went through for 8 years (and 30 before that with family and friends) was from liberal trends.

Donors/lobbyists line up behind Hillary to keep the gravy train rolling and never stop robbing.

Now is the time to ignore everything they say. We've got our man and know he'll save the day.

Never surrender your rights (guns) because once they're gone you'll never get em back (fact).

An armed society is a polite society. Especially if concealed, one never knows so he acts nicely.

Now's the time to just listen to Trump and ignore his detractors. Not wasting time/hurt is what matters.

QUEEN BEE

The same creepy kids needing "safe zones" are wearing Che Guavira shirts--what hypocritical jerks.

This business of not letting millions trickle down to those in need is common with the Clintons.

You can get a Ph.D. in Global Warming though it's all bull and a hoax. Degrees mean nothing now folks.

FIFTY-YEAR LIBERAL NARRATIVE

The liberals have had control of how we think for fifty years and we're sick of it/reversing out of it.

The crazy liberals are arrogant creeps. These are brats who need to have their face slapped I think.

Democrats: Corrupt from the beginning always under the banner of goodness and right (yet a blight).

The Democrats were corrupt from the beginning since they were for slavery, the KKK and other sinning.

The globalist plan through the democrats: make us poor, stupid and controllable (progressive doormats).

Slave owners and the KKK were democrats and Hillary loves them, that hypocritical dem!

Democrats were slaveowners and the KKK--then they switched it: reps were racists, they were ok.

Hillary Clinton is a risk Americans can't afford to take. Don Trump Jr.

Criminals by definition don't follow laws. Don Trump Jr.

See Hillary's America! Democrats were the meanest slaveowners ever--they are criminals!

With the Clintons, nothing is sacred and everything's for sale. Donald Trump

QUEEN BEE

Anyone calling Trump a "racist sexist homophobe" is just parroting the globalist-owned news folks.

LIBERALS ARE PARROTS

The way you've gone along with this horrible dark thing, thinking it's "IN" makes you crap and me king.

The Democrats formally nominated the most scandal-plagued and disliked candidate in their history.

For years the more dirt they got on others the less dirt--though exposed-- stuck to them but no more I wager.

Just because you're black doesn't mean you have to vote democrat. Diamond and Silk

Hill-pocrisy: True to form, her speech was riddled with mistruths, equivocations and lies.

The devil's not a maker--the less they give, they're a taker. Its so sickening with the plot thickening.

We've reached the point of total disrespect and cutting all ties to liberals and their endless lies.

Liberals dress in white to appear pure. They detest the one who wears the dark, though a seer.

We're concerned that this is not a good thing but will it not trigger revolution--a swing?

Why did this miscarriage of justice happen? Because they all have dirt or they plant it on em.

America will either be hammered or Trump will nail it. There is no lukewarm but God can help it.

Please God revive the American spirit. We've been overcome with evil and our dark future, I fear it.

QUEEN BEE

The constitution is a beautiful document. It is so efficient you can fit it in your pocket. Paul Ryan

TREATMENT MEANS DEBASEMENT

"Get the treatment they need" means incarceration in a cold heartless camp and never freed.

"Mental health system" may mean a database of those who won't conform to evil or be debased.

Friends and family must be confronted: did they enable this criminal takeover by how they voted?

Any nation calling good evil/evil good is mad. The contagion of madness shows across the land.

Please God let goodness prevail. These criminals are dark forces and perverted as hell!

At first, patriotism brings scorn. But later, when it costs nothing, they all jump on, like a swarm.

How long before it's old news? Get your life back: think eternally not temporally (blues).

Bottom line of left's love of swine: your enemy makes me love you cuz they're no friend of mine.

Diminished military, confused society, coarsened culture or Trump: renaissance or slump?

Don't get discouraged, the creeps are still in power so course they'll ratchet it up to the last hour.

Cause riots to give cops the best tools to cope, then federalize it all: it's all about control.

Two powers in the world: sword and mind. In the end the sword is always beaten by the mind. Napoleon

QUEEN BEE

Liberals always blame others for what they do. Don't get caught up in their guilt projections (dudu).

THE LEFT PROTECTS MUSLIMS

The left "protects Muslims" by embracing Wahhabism's most sexist standards.

The Canadian is sick but because he looks slick (like Obama) the dumb voters are thick as bricks.

For Obama if there are blacks in prison, its racism. He doesn't consider other factors, ma'am.

One thousand people die a month from TB and our gov does nothing cuz destroying the country is it's thing.

Did the snake trigger the shootings? Yes of course and everyone knows that's why we're losing.

The pea brains who can't think for themselves get it from their music, agitators and other traitors.

Civil war has begun but the police will ban together so as not to be killed one by one and it won't be fun.

We're so sick of the Clintons. The chicaneries and outright robbery by them and all their minions.

Your depression began when told "anything goes". Joy comes from restraint (from one who knows).

Imminent change: a false flag by democrats losing power/gravy train, or Nibiru--one and the same?

Obama's more "presidential" than Trump--no matter that he ruined America/put us in a sad slump.

As soon as the false flag/Nibiru occurs, he'll come for the guns: gangs invade and nowhere to run.

QUEEN BEE

TRUMP DOESN'T OFFEND ONE BIT

Trump doesn't offend one bit it's just the democrat moochers who seek to make him look illigit.

The Khans are the latest grieving victims the Dems use to attack as media obsesses one-tracked.

There's been a turnaround, revolution has begun. The hypocrites lost and the people's desires won.

The enemedia went into "full Soviet" last week. It's part of the criminal machine and denial is bleak.

We will remember later, you awful collaborators--ganging up on the best country's only savior.

When you can't make a dent just retreat til' apathy's spent then return as a good lady or gent.

Donald: don't let their disapproval restrain your speech one bit--ignore them/be yourself: legit!

A rigged system and dishonest media. That's what we're running against: boldface lies or trivia.

To run this country we need a badass with sass. Not these wimps so morally lowdown too (no class).

Democrats are the party of war. Not the republicans--they end wars but are called hawks more.

Obama: Trump's unfit--"doesn't know economics or the constitution"--but look in the mirror you twit.

Trump's making his list of liars and collaborators: the entire old guard and RINO fakers.

TRUMP'S NOT A RACIST YOU TWIT

QUEEN BEE

Trump's handsomer each speech cuz the animating contest of liberty brings out one's best.

Which "F.I." is your home--Feminist Influence (bad) or feminine Influence (makes everyone glad).

We don't have a problem with the constitution just lawless politicians like Hillary Clinton.

President Obama will go down as the worst president in the history of the United States. Donald Trump

Common core is so filthy. How dare you do that to our kiddies--you perverts are shameless and guilty.

Save us father, let Donald begin. In Jesus' mighty name, amen.

You better hope you die or Trump wins. Your whole world will degrade to poverty=nothins'

Eliz. Warren: cute little jackets with Neru collar and 3/4 sleeves won't keep you warm on the streets.

Hillary Clinton would be horrifyingly corrupt as president and a disaster in foreign policy again.

This is our chance to overthrow special interests and restore rule by the people after so much evil!

It's about self-discovery, expansion and enlightenment (genius) vs. tyranny (censured and joyless).

Even if Trump died the movement would go on, for the new lines of revolution have been drawn.

They're all about building their empires not protecting our lives. That's why no empathy, and lies.

Keep the problem going so the money keeps flowing. Even though lives are lost they act unknowing.

QUEEN BEE

KEEP PROBLEM GOING FOR MONEY FLOWING

Millenials blame America for the fix we're in. They don't realize it was the democrats (a trash bin).

The real moral burden lies with those refusing to oppose the frightening candidacy of Hillary Clinton.

Pray to God for our country (pray for Trump). Pray that right prevails and we'll get over the hump.

Booze: fun when it's goin' down but a little later or in the morning life is trashed/you're in mourning.

It was the Golden Girls who debased women into debauchery. For godly ladies it is filth and mockery.

Not true: "men were mean to women in the past". They respected/protected cuz both had class.

Older women go for younger men but have to educate the puppy. It's not a feather in your cap lady.

If the central government becomes destructive of our rights, the second amendment ends the fight.

Henry the VIII Syndrome: Wanting to get rid of wife he accuses her of adultery to ruin/end her life.

Campus carry eliminates kill zones in school. The students can finally rest easy and just be cool.

It's not him it's who he delegates to get jobs done and we have faith he'll choose rightly, each one.

Of course he was trying to destroy this country. There should be no question about this tragedy.

Forget unity: Jesus never came to unite but to divide us from significant others/people who bother.

QUEEN BEE

Trump's the real deal and thus they're throwing everything they've got against him. Alex Jones

AMERICA STARTED WITH GUNGRABBING

The country started when they came to get the guns: added the 2nd amendment, then we won.

Most men aren't leaders, they follow the women. Women make the decisions though lacking vision.

Voting for Trump was the Christian thing to do. For Hillary is a criminal/would've crushed America and soon.

The sands of time that made this country great are running low. Alex Jones

It's a limited democracy--51% can't consign the 49% to slavery cuz it's constrained by law, see?

Charity for some should not compromise security for all. Governor Gregg Abbot

The insanity of liberalism: thinking "everybody's good". They don't see them as evil just "misunderstood".

We lost the 4th estate years ago. Now it's run by monstrous left-wing fanatics hating America as foe.

They hate him cuz he's rich and white. This is a terrible situation since in every way he's right.

They dress nice always with a smile on their face but see past that cuz in a moment they're disgraced.

If God can save us from this it'll be the biggest miracle in history--that's how bad it is, see?

Liberals do nothing about criminals but yell about guns. They are anti-police and all for the thugs.
DEMOCRATS DESTROYED INNER CITIES

QUEEN BEE

Democrats destroyed inner cities and drove out jobs, after ruining the schools and tolerating thug fools.

We have a tinker toy power grid that goes out with inclement weather but about this no one's bitter.

We incarcerate more people than China, a tyranny with 4x the population.

Feminism was never about equal pay but destroying the family. Look higher at the evil purpose honey.

Liberals are wicked and crazy. They wanna let violent criminals go free but kill an innocent baby.

Antifa beat up people praying for peace for both sides. Someone's gonna get killed if unreconciled.

Neat: Due to the structure of revitalization movements it'll now be a mass re-adjustment to a new beat.

You can't act that way/do those things and expect God's blessing (that's the old style of preaching).

Both sides are corrupt but we've got an outsider so both sides hate him, got it?

Both sides hate him and via fake media they've a waged a war of LIES and people bought it/despise.

To please his wife he became a feminist but in truth a sadist cuz that's how it works, it's the gist.

For a man to be feminist means he has to gulp so much untruth he's gonna finally erupt/get cruel.

Wouldn't want men to swing to the other extreme like Taliban but they've been wimped by feminism.

Men take the views of their dumbed down wives who've been brainwashed about how to view life.

QUEEN BEE

WIMPY HUSBANDS TAKE VIEWS OF FEMINIST WIVES

Men want to please their wives, peace at any price. So they agree with this crap and lose their minds.

And they get vituperative too, having lost the ability to think. Razor sharp minds, steel traps of rinkydink.

Rather than studying things deeply they scream insults but it's all so self-discrediting it's funny sort of.

The most popular are meaningless. The social world is clueless and boring to seekers of reasonableness.

Common Core kid books are like pornography. This is trash but we're told it's better than geography.

Liberals will do anything to do conservatives in. They'll defame, wreck and trash their reputation.

This mental revolution is so striking as people collect their thoughts after all the lies they bought.

Cannibus is medical, man. It cures all diseases and keeps us staying happy and thin our whole life span.

Do not concur with youth/immorality just to maintain relationship for that's giving up self/being unfit.

We can't see how bad things really are due to sensory overload and infinite distractions but oh Lord!

Liberals aren't talking about open borders, crime, poverty or threats of ISIS just Trump's tone of voice.

Our leaders call our devolution into moral madness "progressivism" but it's sexual perversion/paganism.

He gives a weak speech quickly and gets paid to then change a critical element of foreign policy.

QUEEN BEE

LIBERALS SEE SHARIA AS PROGRESSIVE

Dumb liberals actually see Sharia as progressive--unbelievably dangerous how they love repressives.

The pressure is building against Barrack Obama and Hillary Clinton across this great and glorious nation!

Stop trying to appease people because they are ultimately unappeasable and that means trouble.

It's not just Clintons but the coordination with corrupt media but Trump can undo this in the meanwhile.

I don't put America down we just have to admit we're captured by criminals before turning it around.

With riots comes Martial Law and crackdown. They're foreign bought but some are homegrown.

Clinton Foundation principal: You accuse your opponent of doing what you're doing, always.

As political gangsterism is normalized in America we see massive Stockholm Syndrome and trauma.

Since the sixties it's fashionable to hate America. Through this strategy liberal fools are globalist tools.

If you weren't voting for Trump were you voting for Hillary? Cuz if he lost we'd have gone right into tyranny.

They must blanket us with nonsense because it's so obviously false and so we won't see their faults.

A famous feminist encouraged her fans to swear and not keep house. Now she's rich, the louse!

Grafters were running for president and no one seemed to care, no wonder we're no longer rare.

QUEEN BEE

LIBERALS SEE IMMIGRANTS AS VICTIMS

Liberals think: Immigrants are the victim. Trumpists think: The victim is the American citizen.

They saw him as creepy, childish, stupid and weak--a limp handshake, demonic, up a creek.

He spent all the money on useless wars and refugees then the infrastructure dissolved by degrees.

Increasingly I relate only to Trumpists. The others are working towards our destruction with fascists.

There is a natural division of labor, don't tell me there isn't. Men work the heavy and women light and steady.

How do you grab victory from the jaws of defeat? God does it because it's His battle--how neat!

Cutting taxes is the return of the "big engine". It's prosperity from competition and that is capitalism.

Progressives suggest we should completely abandon Western values to be PC: more liberal insanity.

Regression into ancient pagan sexuality (Sodom Gomorrah type) they call "good" but ya think we should?

MOST LIKED ARE MEANINGLESS SITES

Quit seeking/pumping up your likes. Don't you know the most popular are usually meaningless sites?

And that's all she wrote. I'm sick of the news, will just sit back and pray that all goes well for Trump.

If they're not on the right side they're on the wrong--that's evil and the demon possessed, hypnotized throng.

QUEEN BEE

Until they're on the right side they're on the wrong--a canyon between us--so put on a new song.

I didn't like your thing on sex. That was way over the mark, a verbal assault and embarrassing as heck!

Shut up about it, get some class. You're socially hypnotized to accept this crap--it's gross and crass.

Most people want to look good and they know they don't but don't know why: It's the food.

SEXUAL ASSAULT: "I'M NOT GOOD ENOUGH"

Women who've been sexually assaulted may become promiscuous believing they're not good enough.

It is easier to fool someone than to convince them they have been fooled. Mark Twain

People don't want to hear the truth because they don't want their illusions destroyed. Nietzsche

Instead of facebook here, I'm happier in prayer. But I always return in fascination to the world's snare.

Give em lip and you're going to jail. People are truckling in fear of government: a fly to a whale.

We're waging the war on corruption by crashing through lies and disinformation. Alex Jones

After eating starch I feel like I ate a couch. It's not my thing but a few nuts seems ok (no ouch).

Fox confirms the left by questioning known liars because they control reality as history's actors.

GANGSTER CULTURE PRIMING FOR PRISON

QUEEN BEE

Gangster culture was CIA-created to prep people for prison populations and inciting divisions.

1964 CIA memo: When they won't tow the line we'll call em a "conspiracy theorist" to undermine.

Cause of violence: Media is told to condone thugism so even country music shows destruction.

I too was victimized by the liberal agenda. It takes years to sort it out after mind messes up in America.

Start the equality thing and it never stops--like the French Revolution more heads are lopped.

Be "good to all" and never making distinctions between right and wrong--false equivalence is our fall.

We have an easy job: just tell the truth. We don't have to tax our memories by lying/faking like you.

Cries of "racism" is the oldest trick in the Democrat book. We're getting sick of these (Hillary) crooks.

Hitlerian harridans are crueler than men. It's cuz it's not their true nature to mimic to that end.

To cover his tracks with Monica Lewinsky, Bill Clinton bombed Iraq. How epic, worse than Barrack.

Politicos, media hacks, broken borders, bloated bureaucracy, gov that doesn't work and high tax.

They think if they chum up with evil it won't come after them but they'll be the first damned people.

8 years of torture from this man--and you're even considering the same thing through Hillary Clinton?

It's beginning to topple then it'll all fall down. That's the way revolution works when full blown.

QUEEN BEE

PATHOLOGICAL LIARS AND THIEVES

A lie told often enough becomes the truth. Vladimir Lenin

I don't think of you as a person of "color" but a person, period. But you divide us and it's weird.

They are too dumb to be scared. The low-information voters are naive, dangerous and unprepared.

We'll really see heresy from here on out. The most ridiculous excuses for sermons, no doubt.

To blacks: Two times we elected the first black president ever and did your condition get any better?

The B.S. we've been taught: I used to hate it too but It was a set up for destruction--to USA bid adieu.

Bullshit race-baiting leftist narratives is all he's spouting. He's a total fool but they're encouraging.

You can't ignore it til it comes on your doorstep. It's happening we're falling but Trump gives us pep.

Anti-flag stuff started in the sixties with the creepy hippies so retrieve happies by returning to the fifties.

It was a national curse when the hippies became sexually perverse and the wages of sin is the hearse.

When liberals say to conservatives "you should mature" it means you should "sell out", for sure.

If you wanna learn about Civics, fine. But if you just wanna argue, shut up you're no friend of mine.

I'm not wasting any more energy arguing with you, low brain! You're dumbed down, a ball and chain.

QUEEN BEE

CONSERVE YOUR ENERGY/MAINTAIN IDENTITY

I've allowed you to eclipse my identity by giving you time in my head but no more for you are the enemy.

We need to take action, the gloves are off. We know who you are and we'll stop you, though you scoff.

No matter what you say you're a "racist", "hater", "bigot" and "homophobe". I tell you this is getting old.

Everything is racist and I mean everything. If their song you don't sing you're a worm/they're the king.

We'll get the jobs back and have school choice. We'll have renewed prosperity and get back our voice.

None of this is reported on the news, all globalist-owned and run. Even FOX has Saudis on the board, hon'.

To blacks: Two times we elected the first black president ever and did your condition get any better?

Why aren't feminists against Islam? Simple: Either they're chicken or don't know what they're sayin'.

More whites are killed by police and black killings are by other blacks but you won't hear those facts.

Black Lives Matter is a fake liberal narrative. Only if you go along do you have your first amendment.

If my free speech doesn't go along with them suddenly it's called "hateful" and "divisive" what I said.

B.S. race-baiting leftist narratives is all he's spouting. He's a total fool but they're encouraging.

They don't even know what they're protesting about. No history, no poli sci, no civics--an embarrassment.

QUEEN BEE

WHO ARE YOUR TRUE SISTERS? GOD-LOVERS

Feminist sisters will hold you down. They don't want you doing your thing and will destroy your crown.

Couldn't care less what you liberals think. You stink so please leave, low-thinkers are rinkydink.

The evil rich have hired whole armies against us. Only Trump can solve if we have any chance.

Christianity, conservatism and Trump support is "intolerant, hateful and racist" on campuses nationwide.

Trump hates the corruption but not the principals: those "principals for which we stand."

You loved that man, you got him in. You enabled this criminal takeover cuz he justified your sins.

Turn it all off and just listen to Trump. He's our only hope, raised by God to get us over the hump.

The progressives are so insensitive they can't empathize with the victims of ideological directives.

He'll call off the dogs--the spies. He can do that for power trickles down--what he says goes/spy dies.

Besides Jesus, Trump is the one giving us hope. Listen to him--a return to reason after that dope.

Marriage is liberation for a woman so she can create, protected from the rabble and the vermin.

When everyone's a prepper and we explode into innovation it's due to Trump's giving us freedom.

No one feels safe, our time is limited. The enemy couldn't care less, they are so arrogant and bigoted.

QUEEN BEE

God is taking the power of speech away from Hillary. What beautiful justice, now to the pillory.

GOD VS. DEMOCRAT'S VOTER FRAUD

The biggest threat is Organized Mass Multiple Voting. Otherwise it's a landslide so I'm praying and hoping.

Shame the anthem-sitters for they're no better it's all about principals/not friends of fair weather.

Even the worst dictators hate traitors (those who treacherously self-deal) and love martyrs.

Right before Kennedy was murdered he had signed documents eliminating the Federal Reserve.

It's the principals for which we stand. Not whether you're happy with the people in this great land.

Creeps who can't think join in: sitting during our national anthem despite those who died and it stinks.

Great jobs, great neighborhoods, honesty restored. Embrace it: the party of Abe Lincoln and more.

Safety again. Like our childhoods in America: that's after Obama and four decades of trauma.

Jobs will return, prosperity will arise and manufacturing will snap back from every country. Donald Trump

The "sexist racist homophobe islamaphobe hater/bigot" thing has gone too far--they block your star.

Hardening: Taking the velvet glove off the iron fist is a sign of weakening so take heart though bleeding.

When our New Day comes all collaborators, traitors and gophers will be arrested immediately, no worry.

QUEEN BEE

When does your social justice stand as warrior become just an apologist for violence and murder?

Revitalization Movements show all through history. Led by a charismatic leader it's sudden victory.

REVITALIZATION MOVEMENTS AND NATIONS

Revitalization Movements rejuvenate nations as we see mass readjustment to a new beat.

It was like being stuck in a sewer: You didn't know any better and demons blocked just cuz you knew her.

He speaks the truth. Every word drips with common sense, logic, strength and fighting for patriots, the few.

They think if they can come up with a label for something it becomes reality. How ridiculous, really.

Thirst for Blood: The Revolutionary kills the opposition but then his own (counter-revolutionaries) and it goes on.

Prosperity will rise, poverty will recede and wages will then grow rapidly. Donald Trump

White Guilt: But 95% of murders of blacks are by other blacks! But the BLMs refuse to listen to that fact.

He refused to stand. He disrespected all those who died to ensure freedom in our great land.

Many of you have put down America for years. You bought the LIE/enabled a criminal takeover of tears.

The corrupt media and leaders are falling apart publicly. This will be over soon so persevere gratefully.

Hillary wants to kill babies days before delivery by pulling them apart: it is so grizzly/this woman is shady.

QUEEN BEE

LOSE RESPECT FOR FANS OF TRASH

Lose respect for those blindly following this shady lady. You must for your own sake/to be happy.

Hillary wanted to kill babies two days before delivered. Now, how can you possibly not hate her?

Don't pity those who disrespected and left you alone/forlorned and ruined your rep too, just get armed.

Love those who love you--your True Self is so cool but unfortunately banned by the cruel.

Mental illness/lost genius sets in adapting to nuts. Lost soul: gotta learn to hang on or flunk.

Feminist friends want you divorced. Due to liberalism/globalism that's how far our culture's morphed.

If God raised him up He will also protect him. Hallelujah Lord, fill his cup and banish his foes nonstop!

The only people mad at you for speaking the truth are those living the lie.

Ban her, lock her up for public indecency, put her in mental asylum: How does she get away with this man?

Michelle Obama is the most vulgar first lady we've ever had. Mike Pence

How could you vote for Hillary when she wants to kill a near-infant baby--are you crazy or evil maybe?

In times of war the laws fall silent. Antonin Scalia

Liberalism has been the default setting up to now, with this landslide revolution which is mental.

Americans are the most inventive people on the planet. When Satan rushes in we always solve it.

QUEEN BEE

Americans are innovators and thus we came first: Making God central He blocked the curse.

DIRTY SECRETS OF THE POWERFUL

Julian has exposed the dirty secrets of the powerful: Gross brutality and lawlessness called despicable.

As nations lose liberties and go under tyranny we need whistleblowers so don't treat em terribly.

I can't even blame the liberals who messed with my head. They held their line and my spirit went dead.

The military must know an epic false flag is imminent and are readying (secretly diligent), no?

If you steal a landslide it'll mean war. That many people disappointed--OMG, blood and gore.

Why does she look so mean? What kinda image is she trying to portray--a vindictive brawling wife ain't ok!

The harvest is ripe for evangelism to this generation. They're so dumb it's a turkey shoot, amen?

The guest list is modest but the wedding is historic. Marriage changes life completely/makes one heroic.

Disrespect for cops starts at the top. Even fire fighters are shot--need Trump not these despots!

I can't imagine what would happen if she stole the election: At this point of Trump-hysteria? Destruction.

He doesn't drink, he doesn't smoke. He's gonna fix our system: put it on the right track/remove the yoke.

People in this country are fed up with stupidity, weakness and not beating ISIS.
Donald J. Trump

QUEEN BEE

We're winning no matter what you hear from the media: thieves and crooks. As bad as Hillary: kooks.

CORNY COMICS PAID BY GLOBALISTS

Without the corrupt media and corny comics Hillary would be nothing whether politics or economics.

The highest is a preacher to preachers/teacher to teachers. One at a time then they go out there.

Deport criminal illegal offenders quickly--that's the National Security Act, ignored completely.

They'll recall you were always for Trump (before he was popular) and you'll rise up as an officer.

Now we find out Obama stole his election. Dear God, all that time, decline, ruination, loss and destruction!

Either she loses and goes to jail or she becomes queen of the New World Order and criminals prevail.

NFL: One tattooed idiot throwing a ball to another tattooed idiot and that's called "civilization", believe it.

The best laid plans of mice and men often go awry. Robert Burns

Childlike minds really believe that Obama and Hillary are their friends and want to help em.

They want you broke, destitute, failed. They want you unsuccessful and it's planned in great detail.

They are hypocrites of the worst kind. Sick degenerate users/moochers and fools: Satan's tools!

Michelle Obama's guests wrote songs about raping women and she dared to say Trump's the vermin?

QUEEN BEE

Just imagine if Trump were hanging out with rappers bragging about date-rape of drugged women!

LASCIVIOUS LIBS SEXUALIZE KIDS

Here they sexualize our kids with trash then demonize Donald Trump for it-- just wait for our backlash!

I hate to say we hate but after 8 years of trauma how could we not be irate made to accept this fate?

She's just another silly female on the left--she knows nothing so by default ends a liberal: daft.

Remember what I told you: That if Trump got in, it would be the opposite to what it's been: rich/fun.

Hillary gave them fifteen hundred dollars and an Iphone: "Go to Trump's rally and beat people up—come on"

Them stealing the election is a huge victory as well, since it further discredits them. Alex Jones

Fox has become lackluster/boring compared to the true headlines with proper priorities assigned.

FOX is filled with boring details, speedbumps like Williams or feminist like Kelly--YUK! Fox sux!

Here we're sinking and Kelly's talking about women's feelings. Feminists are stupid and frightening!

On the one side is greatness and hope, on the other is silliness, false narratives and pettiness by dopes.

Here we're facing the razor's edge--of returning from the brink or sudden sink- -and feminists just wanna bitch.

It's the women who are for Hillary Clinton. It's identity politics: that's how shallow and superficial their thinkin'

QUEEN BEE

FEMINISTS ARE THIRD RATE THINKERS

These feminist are third-rate thinkers. They can't see the whole and mess everything up: messers/stinkers.

They lack tenderness, our feminine part. They are cold and heartless and many are little tarts.

The most foul, out-of-control date rape lyrics and more. That's in the Whitehouse/it's a cultural war.

Megyn Kelly is a stab in the back. Feminist hypocrisy hurts sensitives as we face nuclear war (fact).

These crazy feminists will take us into war! Putin wants to be friends but has his line then he'll roar.

A man in the wrong can't stand against a man in the right who keeps on coming. Founder of Texas Rangers

Let justice be done though the heaven's fall. (Fiat justitia ruat caelum, Latin legal phrase)

Hillary is a known warmonger: the pentagon warned us. Very unstable—a vote for her is war (it's nuts).

A billion to take him down won't matter if a landslide later, as God raises standard against God-haters.

They're incompetent and have no common sense while enforcing a sick will which ruins lives/makes us dense.

From liberalism (A sick mean debauched dumbed/wimped culture) you can escape through Trumpism.

What about that sick devil pres. of Canada, Trudeau? He's just as perverted by liberalism from below.

HILLARY WANTS TO KILL PRE-NEWBORNS

QUEEN BEE

Hillary wants to kill (two days short of) newborns. Think of that--it's her worst crime/she is abhorrent.

As it all comes out we've no more reason to pout cuz vindication is here so let out a shout!

Enantiodromia is occurring: That's when the bottom becomes the top and the top is self-destroying.

An inversions of systems is happening as we speak. That's where we win and the foe's up a creek.

Voting a third party is voting for Hillary--can't anyone think deeply?--but even the Mormons are this silly.

There is no tenderness in her steely-steady face. There is only shame, corruption and utter disgrace.

How wonderful as we've won and after trouble (a ton) our eyes go out to our future's beautiful horizon!

What a time to be living. Hypocrisy is crashing and prosperity's just beginning as that dark cloud is leaving.

In exchange for amnesty for multiple felonies Huma will be forced to testify against her rejecting lover Hillary.

Organized money is just as bad as organized mob. Donald Trump

We had to go through Obama (to see what we don't want) and it was a trauma but now we've found Trump nirvana.

Don't gain the world to lose your soul, wisdom is better than silver and gold. Bob Marley

We watched the kleptocrats dismantle America and now we want her back. We weren't watchmen/we were lax.

All bull feminism always ends up looking dumb! We're onto you and it's weakness/inferiority (crumbs).

QUEEN BEE

The church has turned us into patsies so the bullies run right over us. That's from being "nice": stop this!

ALL-BULL FEMINISM LOOKS DUMB

We've gone from a melting pot to a chamber pot in one generation. Michael Savage

The archetype of the female pedophile is a bottomless pit and it's horrible to think about/sick as it gets.

Hillary is making it a women's issue about Trump. Just imagine that but if the college kids believe it we're sunk.

They're training us to accept less, lowered expectations, a new dark age: a post-industrial world/feeling caged.

Hillary's Female Pedophilia: We've come to the line--will we accept this as we did all else that was vile?

Weiner is ready to sing like a bird to send Hillary/Huma down the river: no honor with thieves when God delivers!

Trump supplies the catalyst for a world (not just a national) revolution: (Joy, no more revulsion)!

It's not only Clinton but the death of our history--rewriting all of it since the sixties/influence of hippies.

Men should rule the roost not concede to their feminist wives who scare with vicious gossip/lies.

Anyone who feels deeply--who doesn't have a seared conscience--would be horrified, honest.

By controlling speech they dull our mind and crush our spirit but we can still joyfully pray in private.

You fight for your country and come back being called nazi? It's what's happening in land of the free.

QUEEN BEE

FAKE NEWS: PROPAGANDA FOR AN AGENDA

Daddy Trump--the man who has never let us down yet--has signaled everything's gonna be ok friends.

Fake news doesn't tell us what's happening but implant propaganda cuz they have an agenda.

It's all conjecture, not actual facts. False equivalencies with an agenda and that's the news even FOX.

They're dead in the head due to drugs, food, sin and false ideas and thus repentance returns to bliss.

It's not news it's political slants.

Talking lies, omitting or slanting facts is an attack on your country.

The new hate crime is "demeaning dignity"--but that's so subjective it's just means more tyranny.

Laissez-faire attitude of free will: It all looks like hell cuz it's not of God since you do what thou wilt.

Since God is not dirty disorder you're made in the image of the devil and you can't deny it either.

There is crap everywhere, total disorder like a bomb hit it: Does this reflect God, is it spiritually legit?

Christians can't lie (e.g. about gender) so what's it all about: compelling a lie as we're thrown asunder.

The devil conquered our wonderful country in the sixties and the government are grandkids of those hippies.

Since God raised him up He will also protect him: The savior and fixer of our great country, amen.
Daily our senses were offended, our morals invaded, our logic inverted, our hearts broken and dreams faded.

QUEEN BEE

As soon as they say they're for Hillary you gotta act as though it's Nazis and escape the matrix speedily.

Hillary Clinton, the totalitarian operative under left cover, has fooled us for 40 years but now it's over.

FEMINISM MAKES WIVES COLD

She loved you but feminism made her cold: she accepted the unacceptable (did what she was told).

She was so sweet until she went off to college. Then she was mean, dogmatic, calumnious, horrid.

Those under feminists are driven to mental illness and I can attest to that, self-esteem was a mess.

No worry, returning from the brink is biblical, man. God always shows up at the last minute, then bam!

I see the callousness of liberals in myriad examples that killed the spirit of an angel/blocked channels.

He was shattered by divorce until I said "it was her feminist friends" and his self-hate changed of course.

Their art is silly, meaningless, political, socially hypnotic, pat, redundant, mundane, bland and corny.

Feminists ignore Bill Clinton's rapes and are "shocked" by Trump. What blatant/ignorant hypocrisy: chumps.

Their glowing reviews are pseudo-intellectual and just for attention. It's embarrassing to know them.

In a dumbed generation it matters not how many "likes" cuz smarts are rare/most are high as kites.

Hillary's rallies were smiles, kisses and hugs. Typical female stuff but NO substance/plans, just crud.

QUEEN BEE

Because of who he is inside and the character of the man, this great leader is devastatingly handsome.

HANDSOME LEADER BY WHAT HE DOES

We'll never forget you loved Hillary--the baby killer right before delivery! You'll face justice for this treachery.

The dreaded white male is so evil he gave most of the world everything he had. Alex Jones

Social conformity is a demand of the left. They hate individuality (True Genius) and thus aren't blessed.

Michelle Obama hosted people who promote date-rape and gang-rape but she says Trump is morally base.

At the heart of this election was a simple question: Would the people govern or suffer more corruption?

You gotta wall up cuz wicked men want in your house. But if you're a weak woman you'll let em in: ouch.

The lyrics of Whitehouse rappers were: cop killing, drug dealing, date raping and violence against women.

Put a weak woman in power and as the wicked take over your lives will change forever and get worse every hour.

Liberals deliberately create messes/destroy precious things--gives them a thrill/their evil heart sings.

One candidate was corrupt in political correctness, the other just stuck to the truth, stating the obvious.

Americana that was the wonder of the world is rising like a phoenix right now. Trumps winning: wow!

HEALTHYMINDEDNESS

Same length as our kittens. Cute as can be and carefree. Having long hair has NEVER made sense to me.

The female lockdown buzzcut is chic, elegant, sophisticated, courageous, futuristic, scientific, TRULY liberated.

Have liver or age spots? Don't worry man. With intermittent fasting everything irregular is reset/wiped out.

These people are cruel. Don't let them into your life, your home, around your pets or esp. your children.

100 KAREN KELLOCK BOOKS

AFFINITY OR MISERY
AGELESS CORNUCOPIA
AMERICA AWAKE!
AMERICA'S DAFT ERA
ARTS OF PALEO FASTING
AUTOPHAGY ON CHEATERS
BACKSTABBING NEUROTICS
BETRAYAL TRAUMA
BOOMERS AND BROKENNESS
BOOT ON NECK
CHAMPION GUIDES
COMMIE NUTHOUSE
COMMIES
COMMUNIST SPIRIT
CONTAGION OF MADNESS
CONTAGIOUS MADNESS
CULTURE CLASH BASHED
DAFT LEFT
DAILY FASTARIAN
DAM RATS
DIVERSITY IS CRUELTY
E-RACE WHITE
EVIL FREAKS (Beyond Gross)
THE END OR A BEND?
FEMALE BULLIES AND FEMI-NAZIS
FEMALE CARNALITY
FEMALE DUMB DOWN
FEMALE POWER DRIVE
FEMINISM AND RUIN 1 & 2
FIX FOR MISFITS
FOOLS & TRAMPS
FREEDOM SPEAKING
FRENEMY ENABLER
FRENEMY LIAR
FRENEMY THIEF
FRENEMY TRAITOR
TRENEMY TYRANT
GENIUS IS HELD DOWN
GLOBALISLAM
GOD USES THE FLAWED
HAZE OF THE LATTER DAYS

THE HERD IN WORDS
HIX POLITIX
HOW THEY RUINED US
JUST SKIP DINNER
LE FEMME AND THE COMMUNIST SPIRIT
LIBERAL CHAOS & ROT
LIBERAL DOUBLETHINK
LIBERAL GALL 1 & 2
LIBERAL SHOVE-DOWNS
LOCK YOUR GATE
LOSERS and Femme Fatales
MANUAL FOR SUPERIOR MEN
MODERN ART FROM HELL
MOSTLY FAKE
NOTES TO CHAMPS 1 & 2
OVERCOME FRENEMIES
PC MAKES US CRAZY
PEOPLE ARE CRUEL
PEOPLE PROBLEMS 1 & 2
PERSECUTED GENIUIS
POLI-PSYCH MYSTERIES
PRETENTIOUS SLOBS
QUEEN BEE
RED NEW DEAL
RETURNING TO FIRST NATURE
SEASON OF TREASON
SEPARATE MEANS HOLY
SOCIAL HYPNOTISM
SOLITUDE SOLUTION
SUPERCILIOUS
THE SCHOOLS SCREWED EM UP
TOAD TO PRINCE
TRIALS CYCLES
TRUMP VS. GROUP
TRUST IN TRASH
THE TRUTH ABOUT PEOPLE
UNDERHEANDEDLY CLEVER
WALK TALL WITHIN WALLS
WE'RE NOT ALL ONE
WINNERS SKIP DINNER
WORK OR SMERK

AUTHOR BIO
Karen Kellock Ph.D.

Ph.D Political Psychology, UCI 1976
Post-Doctoral: UCI Medical School
Department of Psychiatry
Grants NIMH, NIAAA

Ph.D. dissertation "A Systems-Theoretic View of Pathologic Interaction" made an early mark as the "Wife of the Alcoholic Syndrome". Postdoctoral research at UCI Medical, Dept. of Psychiatry on the systems surrounding pathology on NIMH and NIAAA federal grants: *The Contagion of Madness: The Psychology of Neurotic Interaction and Pathological Systems*. Therapy tool Therapeutic Playwriting introduced the play *Mary and Murv: Gruesome Twosomes in the Alcoholic Marriage*. She taught Abnormal Psychology and Pathological Systems Theory at UC and CSU campuses and developed "the Debris Theory of Disease" in five books and website: (www.karenkellock.org): *Champion Guides, Daily Fastarian, Just Skip Dinner, Arts of Paleo Fasting, Ageless Cornucopia. Manual for Superior Men is a* pick-it-up-anywhere book that you can't put down (20,000 Kellockialisms) and ever on your desktop it should be found (or this Ebook for superior wordsearch of new jargon).